REFINE YOURSELF

REFINE YOURSELF

Cultivate & Implement 6 Key Qualities for Enhanced Relationships

DENNIS GARRIDO
and
RAYMOND AARON

First edition published by 10-10-10 Publishing

www.BecomeRefined.com
www.DennisGarrido.com

Copyright © 2017 Dennis Garrido and Raymond Aaron

ISBN: 978-1772771930

Dennis Garrido has asserted his right under the Copyright, Designs, and Patents Act, 1988 to be identified as the author of this work.

All rights reserved. No portion of this book may be reproduced mechanically, electronically, or by any other means, including photocopying, without permission of the publisher or author except in the case of brief quotations embodied in critical articles and reviews. It is illegal to copy this book, post it to a website, or distribute it by any other means without permission from the publisher or author.

Limits of Liability and Disclaimer of Warranty

The author and publisher shall not be liable for your misuse of the enclosed material. This book is strictly for informational and educational purposes.

Warning – Disclaimer

The purpose of this book is to educate and entertain. The author and/or publisher do not guarantee that anyone following these techniques, suggestions, tips, ideas, or strategies will become successful. The author and/or publisher shall have neither liability nor responsibility to anyone with respect to any loss or damage caused, or alleged to be caused, directly or indirectly by the information contained in this book.

Publisher 10-10-10 Publishing Markham, ON Canada

Dedication

This book is dedicated to all who strive for excellence, and have the courage to make any needed changes to better themselves; regardless of the difficulty and challenges they may face.

Table of Contents

Acknowledgements ix

Foreword xi

Chapter 1: I Can't Believe How Things Have Changed 1
    It Didn't Happen Without Help 4
    It's All Gold and Diamonds 5
    The 6 Key Qualities of Refinement 9

Chapter 2: Key Quality #6 Forgiveness 13
    The Ultimate Choice 16
    The Process of Forgiveness 18
    Unforgiveness in the Workplace 19
    A Few Other Things About Forgiveness 22

Chapter 3: Key Quality #5 Communication 25
    Key Elements of Clear Communication 30
    Common Tendencies in Communication 33

Chapter 4: Key Quality #4 Trust 37
- Common Tendencies of Trust 41
- Restoring Trust 44

Chapter 5: Key Quality #3 Care 47
- Caring in Family Relationships 50
- Caring in Professional Relationships 50
- Common Tendencies of Caring 52
- The Cost of Indifference 53
- The Life-Changing Power of Caring 54

Chapter 6: Key Quality #2 Respect 57
- How Does the World See Respect? 59
- What is Respect? 61
- How Does Respect Change the World? 64

Chapter 7: Key Quality #1 Love 67
- Four Types of Love 69
- A Life Without Love 72
- The Work of Love 73
- Don't Give Up 75
- In the Name of Love 75
- Where is the Love? 77

Chapter 8: Refinement 79
- The Work of a Lifetime 83
- It Starts Here 90

Acknowledgements

I express gratitude and deep appreciation:

To Raymond Aaron, who not only co-authored this book with me; but also, is my publisher and mentor whom taught me many valuable lessons and motivates me to be all that I can be.

To my book architects; Barbara Powers, who helped me start this book and proved to be my light when I was in the darkness of discouragement. Liz Ventrella, who continue this journey with me and ensured that it got completed.

To Naval Kumar & Chinmai Swamy, whom have helped me navigate the other avenues of this amazing journey that I have been on, and continue to encourage me to carry on and move forward.

To Loral Langemeier, who gave me and Raymond the honour of writing the forward for this book.

To Kim Thompson-Pinder our collaborator and editor; whom assisted us in getting our thoughts into words; enabling us to produce the manuscript in a timely fashion.

Refine Yourself

To Amit and Swapna Ambegaonkar, who inspire me with their amazing example of adaptability, determination, industriousness, and resilience.

To my family and friends, for their love, encouragement and generosity.

Foreword

Have you ever wondered if there was a secret to successful living? Do you watch others live happy, fulfilled, even joyful lives while yours seems blah and ordinary? Do you want to learn something that could help you? Yes, you do. Dennis Garrido and Raymond Aaron have captured it brilliantly in *Refine Yourself*. You may struggle every day because you don't understand that it all comes down to the relationships in your life.

Refine Yourself covers the 6 Key Qualities that are essential for relationship growth and living a fulfilled life. This book is filled with practical examples that help you easily apply what you have learned.

If you are just learning what it means to refine yourself, you will find this as an invaluable guide that will take you step-by-step through the process. You will not only learn what it means to change yourself on the inside but how to apply it to your personal and professional relationships.

If you are well on the road to refinement, you will find this a refreshing read that will not only confirm how far you have

Refine Yourself

come but will give you tools to help others who may need your help in the refinement process.

I recommend this book to you to take your life to the next level and develop long-lasting, profitable relationships both individually and in your career as well. Read this book from cover to cover. You will be so glad you did!

—Loral Langemeier
New York Times Bestselling Author
of *The Millionaire Maker*

Chapter 1

I CAN'T BELIEVE HOW THINGS HAVE CHANGED

"The pessimist sees difficulty in every opportunity. The optimist sees the opportunity in every difficulty."

—Winston Churchill

Have you ever known an extremely pessimistic person? Someone who walks into the room and immediately you start to feel down? You know the moment that they open their mouth everything that comes out will be negative. It can be the most perfect day you have ever had, and they will find a way to make you feel depressed and horrible by the time they leave.

I hate to say this, but I WAS that person. I rarely would see the positive side of things. I always thought the worst of both people and circumstances, especially when anything went wrong.

I would very rarely see what I could learn from the situation or what I did to cause this outcome. I wasn't taking responsibility for my actions. I would always find ways to blame everyone but myself for the terrible things that would happen to me.

Regarding my relationships, I was always pre-judging people. Anytime someone would give me a compliment, or say/do anything nice towards me, my mind would automatically say to itself, "they didn't mean that. What is it that they want from me?" Every kind word, every kind act wasn't genuine; there must have always been an ulterior motive behind it.

It was a horrible place to be. Even though I longed for happiness, I couldn't break the habit of seeing everything in a negative light. I couldn't understand why others had joy and peace and all I had was misery.

BUT...

Thankfully, I am not that person anymore. Now I can truly say that I live an awesome life. I have remarkable relationships both personally and professionally. Phenomenal people are outpouring into my life along with amazing opportunities. My life has truly transformed and I am enjoying the great things that I have.

It Didn't Happen Without Help

Have you heard the saying; "When the student is ready the teacher will come?" That is what happened in my life. When I was ready to make the change, I had phenomenal mentors come into my life to show me how to transition.

The first one I connected with is Raymond Aaron, co-author of this book. He really helped me to see my potential and aim high. He helped me to build confidence in myself and see my value - basically what I have to offer the world. I am so grateful that he helped me see all of that.

Then there are Amit and Swapna Ambegaonkar. They are an exemplary couple who motivate me to keep going and never give up, regardless of what challenges I may face. They came from India to Canada and had to face challenges. Yet, did so with such grace and joy. They are raising two amazing kids; their daughter who is in her early teens, has already written a book; and their young son who likewise is a remarkable child. Just being around this family inspires me to become more.

Jim Rohn teaches that you are the average of the five friends you spend the most of your time with. I came to realize that if I was going to *refine* myself, I had to change the culture around me and I did.

The group of people I associate with now exuberate and send out such positive energy that it uplifts me, encourages me, and empowers me to move forward. I am not to give up, but rather continue to think with a positive attitude and mindset. They are great examples for me to imitate. Through them I see that I have a bright, phenomenal future of abundance, potential, and opportunity. There are remarkable things lying ahead for me. My future is filled with astounding possibilities.

It's All Gold and Diamonds

What does it mean to *refine* yourself? For me it is seven simple words; 'To improve myself by making small changes.' Sounds easy, right? You would think so, but the refinement process in a person's life is similar to that of what gold and diamonds go through to become valuable.

Both of them require intense heat for a period of time

to make them pure. They also lie dormant in the ground, waiting and hoping to be found but then the extraction process begins and they are ripped out of the ground.

The gold is not happy about that. It liked lying in the ground, comfortable with all his gold friends. While life wasn't amazing, it certainly wasn't horrible either. It was always the same and the gold liked it that way. Now he was being torn from everything he held dear and had no clue of what the future held. Maybe it would be exciting, maybe some King or Queen would see him and want only him for that special ring they were thinking of. Who knows, maybe he will be on display for the world to see and admire. The gold started drooling just thinking about it.

But wait. "Where are they taking me? This doesn't look like a castle or a museum. This place is dirty and smelly, and why is it so HOT in here? I don't like this at all. This is more than I can bear. The heat is changing me. All those things that I loved are being forced out of me and I don't want them to go. Please just make it stop. Make it stop!"

At first the gold resists but as he starts to see what his true, pure self is like, he stops fighting and gives himself over to the process and in the end, comes up as a beautiful piece of jewellery on display for the world to see.

The diamond on the other hand, rejoices when she is finally taken out of the ground. While the gold had a life of leisure, lying around, doing nothing and happy to be a part of that dreary world. The diamond had a rough start.

She formed as a dirty, stinky piece of coal that no one

I Can't Believe How Things Have Changed

treasured or wanted. Her life was filled with intense pressure and heat almost from the moment she came into being. Deep in the earth alone, the heat and the pressure were so much that most days she just wanted to end it all. Silently, up through the earth she moved until one day, there was this tremendous shock and the next thing she knew, she was up out of the ground and for the first time she could feel the sun on her face and as she did all those around her gasped at her beauty and people all over the world wanted her. As the jeweller shaped and polished her, she was so happy because all those years of heat and pressure paid off. She was now precious.

I can personally relate to the diamond. My life started out rough. As a child, I was removed from my parents by the Children's Aid Society and spent many years in the foster care system going from home to home. I spent a lot of time adapting to new environments.

Those environments were made of all sorts of people, from all sorts of walks in life. They all viewed things differently and had different levels of maturity and behaviour. Those were the conditions I lived through and ultimately, what had me open myself up to changing my attitude and mindset. I commenced *refining* myself from being pessimistic to optimistic; seeing the good in people, the good in circumstances, and looking at situations from a viewpoint of "what can I learn from this?" Essentially seeking the silver lining in every possible situation.

Another major challenge I had was forgiveness. Past injuries that certain individuals inflicted on me. Especially

Refine Yourself

in the way I was treated when I was a kid; resentment built inside of me. I had to forgive to be able to move on in life. Obviously at the time, I wasn't happy or grateful for what I went through or what happened to me.

Looking back though, being out of the situation and able to see the results that those situations and circumstances produced, I have a level of gratitude for them. Now that I have seen the *silver lining,* the *positive* of those conditions and accompanying events; I realize that they had a part in shaping the person that I have become. I am a remarkable person that is able to handle and quickly adapt to changing circumstances. I can see the positive in every situation. Even my viewpoint/thought process has been *refined*; rather than thinking that, "this person needs to change," or "this circumstance needs to change." I'm taking ownership and responsibility of the situation. I ask myself, "what can **I** do to change that particular situation and make it better?"

Is the refinement process easy? Not usually, especially in the beginning. It can be hard to let go of all those things that need to go, to become the person you are truly meant to be. However, as you let go, as you learn your own value; you come to appreciate the refining process because you know what you need to get rid of and it only makes the rest of you better.

One thing you need to remember, refinement is from the inside out. You can never truly change your actions unless you change who you are on the inside first. The old saying, "Don't judge a book by its cover," is so true. It was easy for me to pretend to be happy, to be enthusiastic and so forth, but deep down on the inside I wasn't.

The 6 Key Qualities of Refinement

As we go through this book we are going to cover the six key qualities that are essential to the refining process. They are like tools that when you first use them they may seem awkward, but as you practice them you become a skilled craftsman. All of them are important and as you implement each one, you are going to notice radical changes in your life. Not only is each one important but they combine as one to make the last key the most effective thing in your life and that is love. Let's take a quick look at all six of them, starting with . . .

#6 Forgiveness

When you forgive it doesn't mean that you forget but you choose to move past whatever injury or hurtful feeling that individual/group caused you. Most people think that forgiveness is an emotion. It is not. It is a choice of your will to let go.

#5 Communication

Communication is what draws people together. The more you get to know people through conversation, the more you are constant, the more you feel closer to that person, and the stronger your relationship gets with that person.

#4 Trust

Trust to me is essentially having a state of mind that is at peace. I can ask someone to do something for me, or tell someone something without fear that they will disclose things I told them in confidence. Essentially, it is a state of mind with very little fear. I know that there may be some troubles in life but I know that things will turn out to my benefit.

#3 Care

Care is to do or say something that uplifts and/or encourages another person, as well as having them feel loved. It is the ability to show love and compassion towards another person even when that person has hurt you.

#2 Respect

Respect to me entails showing honour to another person. That means not bringing up past injuries or holding those injuries against a person (both the person whom inflicted those injuries and any other person). Essentially, treat every person the way you want to be treated and/or to speak to others the way you want to be spoken to. It's about the culture of honour that is so missing in today's society.

#1 Love

The big one is Love. Now the type of love I'm talking about is not the romantic love we see in movies; nor the type of love for a family member or friend. It's rather what is called agape

I Can't Believe How Things Have Changed

love - **unconditional love**. To summarize it, it's altering your mindset, and viewing others as your equal in some sense. Essentially, treat them the way you want to be treated with no prejudice, no judgment, no discrimination, and no stereotyping.

All people have value, because they are human beings. Not just because they happen to be your friends, family members, spouse/partner or someone you like.

When you learn about the power of these qualities and how they work in your life and you start to implement them, you will never regret it. You will be amazed when you look back at how much you have grown and how wonderful your life is compared to what it was before.

I have been through some very difficult things in my life. Including two cardiac arrests within a year of each other, and I learned that if I didn't change there was going to be some serious consequences in my life. I am so glad I did. My life has changed and now it is time for yours too as well. Turn the page and let's get started.

Chapter 2

Key Quality #6

FORGIVENESS

"We must develop and maintain the capacity to forgive. He who is devoid of the power to forgive is devoid of the power to love. There is some good in the worst of us and some evil in the best of us. When we discover this, we are less prone to hate our enemies."

—Martin Luther King. Jr

Alex felt so tense as he walked into the room. Why did he allow himself to be suckered into these horrible family events? Every time he did he spent most of his time hiding from Gary. Why won't he just let it go? That was over two years ago.

Alex had made a mistake that had hurt Gary deeply. He had shared something that Gary had told him in confidence to the WRONG person, who quickly spread it all around the family. As soon as the words came out of his mouth to cousin Julie, the family gossip, he knew he had done wrong. He went to Gary to apologize and make it right but Gary refused to even talk to him. Now, even after all this time Gary still won't even say a word, all he does is glare at Alex from across the room.

It's getting to the point that the family is starting to get involved. Alex is doing his best not to make it a family feud, but every word he says gets back to Gary and just makes the situation worse.

Now Alex says nothing. Hoping that eventually everyone will forget and life can go on. He tries not to let it get to him and keeps a positive attitude in life, but days like today are hard. Why was forgiveness so hard for Gary? Alex wasn't trying to hurt him. He just didn't think before speaking. How can someone live with such bitterness in his heart? His life must be so miserable.

For now, all Alex can do is forgive, go on with his life and hope that one day Gary will change his mind . . .

The Ultimate Choice

Forgiveness. It is one of the things that sets you free mentally and emotionally. Yet, for most people it is one of the hardest qualities to implement in their life. Why? Because it completely goes against our nature. Everything inside of us wants to hold onto our right to be right and have the other person pay for what they did. That's justice, right?

The truth is that justice, like anything else in this world, can be taken to the extreme. Where something that is good becomes something dark that ultimately hurts us instead of helping us. A need for justice can easily become an overwhelming feeling of revenge for every bad thing that happens in life.

The other reason why forgiveness is hard is because of society's attitude towards it. It is thought of as something

Key Quality #6 Forgiveness

only weak people do. They don't understand the mental and emotional strength that comes to you when you forgive.

So, what is forgiveness? For me, it is to stop feeling angry or resentful towards someone for an offense or a mistake. When someone does something, intentional or accidental it is the ability to let go and allow the process of emotional healing to begin. You won't forget right away, but you can make it so that those feelings are not crushing you with their weight.

It is a choice of your will. When something bad happens, it is your emotions that are triggered; that knee-jerk reaction that wants to either run away and hide or come out fighting and hurt them back. Here's the thing, those emotions can lie to you. They tend to exaggerate your perception of the situation along with how you are going to react; and if you allow them to, they can easily overrule logic and sound reasoning.

This is where forgiveness comes in. It is the choice you make to let go of the emotions associated with the hurt. You choose to be peaceful with the person who hurt you rather than allow your emotions to overtake you. Now, I realize this is easier said than done—I kid you not, it is challenging; however, the more you do it, the easier it becomes and the quicker you'll come to realize the benefits.

When you forgive you are not allowing, either consciously or subconsciously, people to interfere with your ability to live and produce results. You will have less negativity when you choose to forgive those people. You will also be able to show honour and respect to that person and not be a cause of division. It opens the door to keep a relationship healthy and it won't affect the people surrounding that person as well.

As I look at the big picture, I can see that ultimately the benefits of forgiving outweigh any bad. In fact, there are no bad outcomes when you choose to pardon someone.

The Process of Forgiveness

I like to think of the process like an onion. There are many layers to it. The first layer is to see the big picture and really determine why you are upset about whatever it is that the person did. Questions that you can ask yourself include:

- Was the action accidental or intentional? Forgiving someone is easier when you know that the person didn't mean to hurt you.

- Is it possible you misinterpreted what the person said or did? For example, somebody said something to you and you felt offended or upset. What was the intention of the person who said that? Did that person mean it in a negative way?

- Are you overreacting? Sometimes if you have been hurt badly in the past such as in the case of abuse, someone might say something innocently but it triggered a memory of something bad and you assumed the person meant the same thing. It is important to analyze what truly happened, not what you thought happened.

Key Quality #6 Forgiveness

The next layer is to determine if it is worth the energy and time to feel what you are feeling? After you have taken a rational look at what happened you may realize that there is nothing to forgive. That it was a misunderstanding and everything is good.

Now, the next layers have to do with actually forgiving someone. The first layers determine if forgiveness is needed. The next layers tell you how to do it.

The most important part of forgiveness is choice. Are you willing to let go of what the other person did no matter what you feel? It all starts with your mind and will, not your emotions. They come later. Sometimes you will be choosing through gritted teeth, and have to fight yourself to do it. That is ok. It doesn't matter how you come to the decision. The crucial thing is that you do.

Now, if what the person has done is serious, you may need to remind yourself for a period of time that you have forgiven them. If it is something minor it is easy to forgive, let go of the emotions and forget. Serious hurts take more time.

The last layer is the hardest and that is being able to treat the person who hurt you with respect and care. That is when you know that you have truly forgiven someone when you genuinely do something nice for them.

Unforgiveness in the Workplace

Most people do not realize the consequences of unforgiveness in their lives. I have this played-out in two main areas; in the family and in the workplace. The funny thing is they both play-out almost the same way. So, let me share a story with you of what can happen when un-forgiveness becomes a habit.

Let me introduce you to Joe. He is working with a group of people on an important project that will result in a million dollars revenue.

One day, outside of work one of his colleagues, Jim, bumped into him and Joe fell down hurting himself. Jim walks off as if nothing had happened.

Now, Joe has a choice to make. He can choose to take offense, be upset, allowing this incident to ruin his day and develop all sorts of negative emotions, or let it go and move on. Joe decides to confront Jim, and does so with the wrong approach. His attitude is harsh and without giving Jim a chance to explain and apologize he attacks him verbally.

Of course, Jim gets upset and a fight ensues. Both leave upset and nothing is resolved and they now have hard feelings towards each other.

The next day, they both go to work. Joe is still steaming that Jim wouldn't apologize, and Jim can't believe how Joe attacked him over something so small. They both go and tell their close associates their side of the story and inevitably getting them on their side. The more people they tell the more that department of the company becomes divided between the two.

Over time as the story gets bigger and bigger, it starts to affect work as people are polarized between the two, and now they don't want to work with each other. Eventually,

Key Quality #6 Forgiveness

because they can no longer work together, the quality drops. It takes longer to get things done, and they lose their million-dollar client. Upper management is not happy and people get disciplined, some even fired.

You can see the massive impact of Joe not choosing to forgive Jim. A group of people who were close friends, now hate each other, and a business is now in trouble.

Let's take a look at the same situation from the viewpoint of forgiveness. Jim bumps into Joe and he falls down. As he gets himself back up, his first reaction was to be angry, but as he caught a glimpse of Jim's face he sees that Jim looks distracted and sad. Joe realizes that Jim probably didn't even know that he had bumped into him, so he shakes it off and forgives him.

The next day at work he goes and talks to Jim and asks him if he is ok? He finds out that his mother had a heart attack yesterday and that it had shaken Jim to the core. Joe offered to help Jim keep up with his work while he deals with his mother's health.

Other people in that department find out about what is going on and they all pull together to make sure that the work gets done. The client is so impressed by the quality of work and how they all helped each other that he gave them an additional two-million-dollar contract which allowed them to expand the company and hire on more people.

As you can see from the just-mentioned scenario, there are substantially contrasting outcomes when it comes to forgiveness. The main lesson here is that a person's CHOICE to forgive or not forgive can have profound impactful results.

Unforgiving causes bitterness, negative feelings, resentment which can easily lead to hatred; cause division among friends, family, and co-workers; as well as limit/reduce your ability to be effective and productive in your day to day activities.

Forgiveness on the other hand not only prevents negative feelings, but also promotes peace, maintains harmony among family, friends, and co-workers. Keeps relationships intact and enables you to be fully effective and productive.

A Few Other Things About Forgiveness

As we come to the end of this chapter there are a few other points I wanted to share with you about forgiveness.

Forgiving is not necessarily forgetting, at least not right away. Forgiving does not mean that you pretend it never happened. Forgiving does not mean that you condone what the person did was right. It is choosing to let go.

One thing I have learned is that as long as I don't forgive I am in-effect hurting myself over and over again as I continually think back to that hurtful experience, and in-essence re-live/re-experience the negative feelings associated with it. When I do forgive all negative feelings associated with that particular hurtful experience gradually disappear.

Forgiveness doesn't necessarily mean that trust is automatically re-established immediately. That comes with time. Like with all actions, there is always a consequence(s)—some pleasant, others not so pleasant.

If someone is continually hurting you, then you need to

Key Quality #6 Forgiveness

set up proper boundaries. Forgiveness doesn't mean that you make yourself a doormat for someone to hurt you again.

Forgiveness also doesn't mean that you have to spend time with people who are angry, abusive, rude or just plain mean. One of the best things you can do in your refining process is to limit contact with those types of people.

Forgiveness enables you to live your life with a more positive outlook. Forgiveness makes it easier to not prejudge people, and overall empowers you to become a better person in the process. Imagine how much more peaceful this world would be if forgiveness was the norm instead of bitterness. Many of the evils of this world wouldn't be able to exist and love would replace hatred.

Chapter 3

Key Quality #5

COMMUNICATION

"Take advantage of every opportunity to practice your communication skills, so that when important opportunities arise, you will have the gift, the style, the sharpness, the clarity and the emotions to affect other people."

—Jim Rohn

Shawn was really nervous about his job interview, so much so that when he was asked about punctuality, his reply was, "I am really good at grammar, especially periods, commas, colons and semi-colons."

Communication is one of the things that makes the world go around, but also one of the areas that is misunderstood on a consistent basis. In this chapter, we are going to look at what communication truly is and how to use it in your refining process.

Simply put, communication is the act of conveying or sharing one's ideas and feelings to an individual or a group. Clear communication is vital in every type of functional relationship. It is essentially what enables the relationship to exist. Communication also enables both the speaker and the listener to comprehend and act on shared goals.

There are different ways of speaking depending on our

relationship to the listener. Think of a conversation you had with a romantic partner compared to one you had with your immediate supervisor. Your relationship roles affected the tone (and content) of the conversation. You also have to take into account the four main styles of communication. Which are assertive, oppressive, passive-aggressive, and submissive.

Assertive communication takes place between two equals. The person speaking has their voice at a medium pitch and speaks at a moderate speed and volume. They can respectfully achieve their conversational objective without hurting or offending the listener. Assertive conversations are enjoyable as both sides feel like they were able to say what they wanted and were also heard.

The oppressive style, by contrast, is spoken in a louder voice with an aggressive tone. Its goal is "to get what the speaker wants to get accomplished," regardless of how others may interpret it. The relationship is not on an equal footing here. Rather, the speaker is attempting to gain dominance over the listener. They are unconcerned as to how others may perceive the tone of the conversation. While the speaker may get pleasure out of it, the listener does not.

Passive-aggressive communication is the mirror to the oppressive communication style. In this instance, one speaker is attempting to hold the dominant role in the relationship, and the other speaker is actively challenging this dominance while maintaining a façade of passive agreement.

The passive-aggressive speaker has the softer, calmer voice patterns of the assertive style, but the message is subtly, indirectly aggressive. The message is often delivered

Key Quality #5 Communication

in an unemotional or controlled monotone voice. Sarcasm is a favourite tool of the passive-aggressive communicator. This style does not facilitate clear communication. It leads to confusion, anger, and resentment. This type of communication often involves trying to manipulate the other person emotionally to get what they want.

Finally, the submissive style is the approach taken by the person who is more apologetic in nature. They avoid confrontation. They find it difficult to take responsibility or make decisions. The tone of voice is softer, and the object of the speaker's message is to soothe or counter any perceived threat of oppressive communication. The speaker has assumed, accurately or not, that they have the inferior role in the conversation. This style tends to lead to frustration on both sides: the speaker feeling anxious and resentful of their inferior role and the listener being exasperated by the wishy-washy acquiescent nature of the speaker.

There are other minor variants on these communication styles, but these are the four main styles we experience on a regular basis. It is useful to become adept at recognizing them. As the listener, it gives us tools to interpret the speaker's goals and motives as well as the message they are trying to convey. Ultimately, our interpretation of the message will determine how we will respond.

The methods by which we communicate will also affect the quality of our messages. People often find they are much clearer communicators in their preferred form of interaction. For example, a writer would find writing letters or emails to be an easier method for conveying their message than producing a video of themselves speaking about the same topic. An actor would prefer to convey the content of their message through a more visual medium (like a video) because it allows for greater emotional nuance.

Key Elements of Clear Communication

The key elements to good communication are respect, tact, and tone. If you want your message to be heard, you must say it in a calm respectful manner. You want to convey your needs clearly and firmly so that you are understood. Your word choice and the tone you use, will tell your listener how important this message is to you. The tone of your voice, your body language, and your facial expressions are the three elements that tell the story of how you view the relationship.

Tact demonstrates an awareness of your listener's needs and feelings. It shows you are a person who considers their words before speaking and extends respect to the listener. Tact is crucial to make sure that you have conveyed your message in a way that the other person can hear and truly understand what you are telling them.

It's a good practice to confirm that your listeners do understand your intent by having the person repeat the message in their own words. This will make certain that you agree on what has been said. Taking the time to ensure both parties are on the same page will help you get to the point quickly.

Let me share a personal story where good communication made a significant difference to me . . .

Key Quality #5 Communication

One time in school, I was assigned to do a group project. I viewed myself as the type of person that people could rely on. I am someone who you can count on to get things done. It's an important character trait to me. However, this trait sometimes can lead to people tending to dump the bulk of the work on me because they know I will get it done and that is what had happened in school.

In this situation, it was a science project. I started to work on the project and I was waiting on one of my classmates to contribute his part of the project. He was not communicating: never getting back to me when I tried to contact him. Finally, I took the initiative and I went over to his place to speak with him in person. We talked in a calm, respectful, tactful manner. I asked him for his part of the project. He was embarrassed to be confronted and began feeding me all sorts of excuses. So again, while keeping my tone even and pleasant, I pointed out, "You know, I likewise have had things that came up. I had other commitments that I had to deal with. There were parts of the assignment that I didn't understand. I found them challenging, but I made sure I found solutions to those challenges. If I couldn't find a solution, I found someone who was able to help me."

I expressed sympathy, but gently reminded him of his own responsibility in a respectful manner. "I am not going to do your work for you. If you need help, tell me what it is that you need, or what parts of it that you do not understand. What parts do you need help with?"

The tactful approach took a little more time, and it took some patience, but eventually, he was able to produce his part of the project. The assignment was well-received and our relationship did not suffer. Good, clear communication feels great and brings people together.

Bad communication, on the other hand, can fracture relationships and tear people apart. I had some clients, a married couple, who were always fighting and arguing. It seemed like they could never find common ground. The wife was verbally aggressive with her husband. She was always finding reasons to attack him. She would call him out, i.e. listing everything she thought he was doing wrong. He would take the defensive approach of, "Why are you picking on me? Why are you behaving like this?" He was playing the victim card, classic submissive behaviour. Technically, they were both playing the victim at various points, but he was the more frequent and defensive victim.

They had a problem communicating with each other. Neither of them were able to clearly convey the daily struggles and challenges they faced as individuals to one another. This left their respective partners unable to empathize and connect with them. He couldn't see that when he didn't do what she asked of him, it caused her to feel hurt and therefore she would verbally attack him.

After they finally started talking and communicating with each other a little better, the husband started to share the challenges he was facing at work or with friends with his wife. That enabled her to be more understanding of his challenges and more patient. Likewise, she conveyed her feelings to him, how she perceived his actions and his non-compliance. Afterwards, when they finally sat down and had

Key Quality #5 Communication

a calm, respectful conversation, they could work things out and move forward, both taking the time to communicate clearly. Obviously, that is not to say that every conversation is perfect, but it is a massive improvement to what it was before. Now that they can better understand each other, they are able to move forward in a partnership, rather than competing for the title of "victim."

Common Tendencies in Communication

Is it surprising to know that men and women have different communication traits? Men often have the idea that they must be macho. That they must be tough and carry the weight of their challenges in silence. Rather than trying to convey the difficulties that cause them to feel powerless or frustrated. Men often don't say anything because they don't want their partners to think of them as weak. This can also be a tendency for women as well, but I see it more frequently in my male clients.

The most common tendency I see in my female clients is that when they express a want, they do it in an indirect manner. Women speak to build rapport, where the main goal is a relationship. They may overexplain a situation, going back over minor details repeatedly in their pursuit of making a relationship connection, before they finally get to the point. By the time they do get to their point, their listeners have tuned-out and stopped listening. This is not to say that some men don't do this as well, but the tendency comes up more often with women.

Conversely, men tend to neglect details when communicating. The macho ideology, says, "It's not manly to express feelings." Men try to speak about what they are going through, the hardships and challenges, but their emotional vocabulary is limited to conveying the message in an aggressive manner. The result is that the listener tends to interpret it as a harsh, attacking diatribe, not a necessary pressure release.

Is he attacking him or her? Possibly. If the way a message is conveyed tends to be very aggressive, it is not conducive to achieving what the person wants. It is not conducive to enabling the listener to understand and accept what the speaker is trying to say. Those are the common tendencies when a man expresses himself in a macho ideology: he represses his feelings, but what he does express he does it in an aggressive, untactful manner--which comes across as an attack on the listener.

Both men and women can fall into the trap of allowing their emotions to overtake the conversation. It is easy to allow emotions to take control of you when you care deeply about something. Emotion can muddle up what you are trying to convey. You don't say what you truly mean to say. You allow your emotions to flow freely and overwhelm, which has you ending up saying things you don't mean or you say things you do mean but you shouldn't say. Your tone will get you into trouble.

While it would be easy to say, "Men and women have different communication traits," and leave it at that, we must overcome these common tendencies if we want to communicate effectively. We must become aware of our own bad con-

Key Quality #5 Communication

versational habits if we want to convey our messages to our listeners with clarity and create lasting relationships.

That's why when it comes to refining yourself to become the best possible you, you need to work on your communication skills.

Chapter 4

Key Quality #4
TRUST

"When the trust account is high, communication is easy, instant, and effective."

—Stephen R. Covey

Trust is the firm belief in the reliability of a person or a system. It is crucial to your daily interactions with the world around you. Think of all the systems and people you trust without even realizing it in a typical day: you get up out of bed, shower, eat breakfast and go to work. At lunch, you bought a tuna sandwich and then worked the rest of the afternoon. You *trusted* that the water would turn on in the shower, that the car would start and that you would be able to buy lunch at the cafeteria. Your life hinges on the fact that these systems and the people responsible are reliable. You depend on that *trust*.

One of the greatest benefits of being able to trust is peace of mind. You experience this peace when you know that what you say to someone in confidence won't be revealed. It's having the reassurance that when given a promise, what was promised will be done. Having a firm belief in a person's reliability gives you the freedom to plan for the future instead of continually making contingency plans.

Trust could also be defined as the self-assurance that stems from knowing that no matter what the situation, that things are still going to turn out well. Regardless of others' actions, even if they don't always come through, you will have done everything you can to achieve your goal. Circumstances may set you back temporarily, but ultimately, you know that you will succeed in the end. You trust in yourself.

But what happens in a relationship when trust is not present? When trust is not in a relationship, it quickly gets off track. It doesn't have to be a large breach to cause problems. Little disappointments, like lateness or forgotten promises, wear away at trust. It is easy for both parties to become overly critical with each other as occasional incidents turn into habit.

Pushed to the extreme, a lack of trust can grow into paranoia. Once distrust has built to the point of paranoia, even the most minor occurrences are suspect. If something doesn't seem right, or if events unfold differently than expected, for example: a husband repeatedly being later than expected when coming home for dinner—his actions plant the seeds of distrust. After a period of similar infractions, his wife doesn't trust her husband's reliability and she starts wondering what other promises he might be breaking. As the saying goes, "If someone can be trusted with little things, he can be trusted with great things." Unfortunately, the reverse is also true. That tendency creates the breeding ground for paranoia to occur.

Key Quality #4 Trust

Common Tendencies of Trust

When any new relationship is formed, trust is usually understood to be granted until the individual or individuals prove otherwise. But once trust has been broken, then it must be regained. Trust must be re-earned by proving oneself frequently with several small actions over time. Picture trust that someone has in you like a savings account with a healthy balance, say $5,000. Imagine that a thief accessed your account and drained it down to a few cents. You would be very upset! Broken trust is like that ransacked bank account. Restoring the balance to its original state will take work.

Value the trust people have in you. People regard trustworthiness based on past behaviour. Honour your words and keep your promises. It's better to under-promise and over-deliver than to disappoint. Building an impeccable character is crucial to the process of *refinement*.

When a new relationship is made, a basic level of trust is naturally established. We unconsciously assess in our minds whether we can trust someone, based on short conversation and some unspoken behaviours. Body language, especially eye contact, can also play a role in how much trust we place in a person.

The common tendency with trust is to extend a basic level to people because of socialization: as children, we are taught that society works best when we consider the goodness of others. Therefore, a helpful, friendly person appears to be working toward the shared goal of common good, which aligns with our personal goals, causing us to want to trust them.

Let's say I meet Robert Carlson, a roofing contractor, at a meeting for local entrepreneurs. He smiled and looked me in the eye as he shook my hand. Since he is friendly and seems sincere, I begin to trust him. Our meeting is perfect timing, because I need to get my roof fixed after a heavy storm tore-up some shingles. Robert tells me he can give me a free estimate on the job sometime next week. I'm happy to work with a local contractor, so we exchange business cards and I wait for his call.

After a few days pass, I decide to call him. He explained that he overbooked and would get back to me by the beginning of next week. *No problem. Anyone can get busy,* I think to myself. But when I don't hear from Robert until late on Thursday afternoon, I begin to question his reliability. At this point, I don't believe that Robert is avoiding me, or lying, but he has not kept his word about a simple phone call. *How can I be sure about what he says about my roof?* The level of trust I placed in him has been reduced.

Subconsciously, I start building a case whether my original assessment is valid or if I can't trust Robert. This doubt leads to the tendency of me becoming overly critical of everything that Robert says or does. The problem with that is Robert could recognize that behaviour in me and the relationship may become strained. Where there is strain in a relationship, conflict can arise.

Another common tendency of trust is periodically reassessing the level of trust you have placed in a person based on

Key Quality #4 Trust

additional information and further interactions. If the information is negative or unpleasant, you may start reducing your level of trust in this person. Eventually reaching a point where conflict can result, or even a complete dissolution of the relationship. If the information is pleasant and positive, trust grows and the relationship bond is strengthened. Let's consider a simple example of how trust can be displayed in a relationship.

Janice has a good friend at work, Joel. They are often assigned to work together closely. Now, Brad, Janice's husband is aware of this pairing and has met Joel himself. Janice tends to spend a lot of time with Joel, both at work and casually. When Brad does see them together, he remains unconcerned, because he trusts his wife.

Then, circumstances arise where Janice and Joel must take a work trip for a conference. When they arrive, they discover an error has been made and they are booked in the same hotel room together. Janice clears the misunderstanding through the concierge and a second room was reserved. Later that night when Janice called Brad to say goodnight, they both laughed at the incident because the hotel gave her a voucher for the hotel restaurant as an apology.

Since he truly trusts his wife, Brad knew his wife would be thinking about her presentation at the conference. Rather than harbour any unfounded suspicions or concocting imaginary scenarios that paranoia would helpfully supply, Brad started thinking about the kind of romantic scenarios that he would enjoy sharing with his wife. He made a reminder note on his phone to meet Janice at the airport with flowers and to make reservations at her favourite restaurant to let her know that he missed her. When she came home, Janice was really impressed to see that Brad had fixed the leaky faucet while she was away. In fact, she showed him just how much *she* missed him!

Restoring Trust

But how do we restore trust when it has been broken? We are only human and despite our best intentions, at some point we will find ourselves in a situation where we are guilty of letting someone down. If you find yourself needing to repair a relationship damaged by broken trust, you must begin the process of reconciliation.

The first step to reconciliation is to take responsibility for your part and admit that your actions have damaged trust. If I have broken trust with someone, I acknowledge the wrongdoing and apologize. Please note that the person who is seeking forgiveness *does not get to decide whether their actions hurt the other person*. (If I stepped on your toes, I wouldn't say, "What are you complaining about? My foot feels fine!" If they say they were hurt, believe them!)

After apologizing, ask for forgiveness. These are two separate steps. Many people think that saying, "I'm sorry," is the equivalent to asking for forgiveness, but it's not. It is an expression of regret, not an indication that the person wants to repair the damaged relationship. Ask to be forgiven, and remember that forgiveness can take time.

If my friend is willing to forgive me, then I must earn

Key Quality #4 Trust

his trust back again and that takes time. I can't expect or demand that person trust me when I want them to trust me. I must recognize they are processing their feelings and remain humble. It is tempting to want to fix things as quickly as possible, but trying to "hurry things along" will not re-establish that trust. I must begin again, being honest and straightforward with the person whose trust I lost. I must convey that I am truly sorry, that I truly do want to gain their trust again.

When my friend is ready to accept my apology, I would look for opportunities to prove myself to him. Starting with little things at first. I have to prove that he can safely trust me in those small things. Then once I prove myself trustworthy in those small things, I can gradually move on to being trusted in bigger things. Always remembering that this reconciliation process is an investment that could take months, even years.

Wait a minute. I could be waiting years? Yes. I can't complain if that is how long it takes to fix the problem. It is unfair to hold that against the person when I am the one that screwed up. I am the one who betrayed their trust. Frankly, I don't have the right to make demands or expect them to trust me again. This is where you are refining your character. Doing the challenging work of being patient and humble. If it is to repair the broken trust of a close friend, or a spouse, it is always worth the effort.

What if the person doesn't forgive me for betraying their trust, even if I have been patient? Remind yourself: I am the one that made the decision to betray their trust. I have to

Refine Yourself

live with the consequences. I must do my best to squelch any hard feelings that I may have due to the fact my friend is not willing to forgive me. Also, I must keep in mind not to let those negative feelings affect my ability to do what is right.

If my friend doesn't forgive me for betraying his trust, I *still* must do everything I can to gain his forgiveness (though it's important to maintain reasonableness). Why? Because if you are truly serious about refining yourself, you must do the work to become impeccable with your word. This is the only way to become a person of integrity.

Trust shouldn't be taken for granted. If we are blessed enough to have it, we should cherish it. We should do everything we possibly can to hold on to it. If we do mess up and lose that trust, we must be humble.

Don't let resentment build when a person is reluctant to trust. Consciously decide that you refuse to allow those feelings to develop. Remind yourself, "I am at fault here. I am the one that created this situation. I am the one who lost that trust. Actions have consequences."

Even if you do face the painful situation of having to heal a relationship damaged by broken trust, don't lose hope. You are refining yourself and becoming the diamond that you were meant to be.

Chapter 5

Key Quality #3
CARE

"Never believe that a few caring people can't change the world. For, indeed, that's all who ever have."

—Margaret Mead

Care is the act of showing genuine interest in someone and doing everything that you possibly can to ensure that the person knows that you do have a sincere personal interest in their wellbeing. Sometimes, people are unable to perceive that you truly care because they are too wrapped up in their own immediate concerns to recognize that you genuinely care for them. When you care about someone, you pay close attention to their interests and priorities too. The key focus is doing everything you can to express your care in a way that is meaningful to them, both through your words and your actions.

Caring allows people to cope with life's challenges. Knowing that they have the support of someone who cares about them enables a person to persist, to press forward, and conquer those challenges. Caring inspires hope for a better future. Knowing that there is someone willing to stand by their side. In return, the person showing care feels good in demonstrating their affection for another person. It keeps people together and creates a powerful bond.

Refine Yourself

Caring in Family Relationships

A simple example of caring in a family relationship is showing personal interest in another person, like asking, "How was your day?" and giving a listening ear. Put the focus on the other person. If you notice the person is not behaving like their usual self, give them the space to share their feelings without being insistent or intrusive. Listening and thoughtfully responding to show personal interest, ensures that the person knows that you care.

For example, imagine a parent picking his child from school. The father could ask his daughter, "How was your day? What was the best part of your day?" This second question is powerful for building a close relationship, because he is asking her opinion and helping her find her own voice. He could find out who she played with. Whether she likes her teacher, or maybe simply the ride home with Dad is the highlight of her day.

Take the time to ask your family about what is important to them. Pay attention to the things that make them happy, or sad, or even angry. You will learn about their character, their passions, and the things they value most in relationships.

Caring in Professional Relationships

It is vital to show care in your professional relationships for many reasons; it shows that you respect and value your colleagues and their contributions and you are part of the team. Being aware of their personal interests demonstrates

Key Quality #3 Care

that you recognize them as unique individuals. Each bringing their own gifts to the table. When you work with colleagues that you also view as your friends, you are more invested in seeing the group succeed.

If you notice a behaviour change in a colleague, your first instinct might be to ask questions to show that you care. It is beneficial to assess the level of intimacy you have in the relationship before you inadvertently pry. Consider the usual depth of conversation you would have with this person. Do you talk about your personal lives (hopefully at lunch)? Or, are your exchanges limited exclusively to work-related topics? Do you spend time together outside of work?

If you do not have a relationship that goes beyond professional courtesy, it would be insincere to ask them to volunteer intimate personal details. Depending on the work environment, it might present the speaker with yet another problem: will a personal crisis turn into a professional liability? Rather than caring, your questions might seemingly have you perceived as coming across as intrusive and rude. How can we address the issue without feeling as though we are overstepping boundaries? Better to err on the side of caution and restrict your inquiries to tactful observation. Such as, "You seem frustrated today. Is there something bothering you?"

Your goal is to convey empathy and a solution-oriented approach. You are concerned about both their feelings *and* their ability to carry-out their job. They are part of a team. A part of the company, and that production (or lack of it) can affect you and your work. Look for ways to assist them without taking over too much of their job for them, and motivate them to do their part. Encourage them as they work on their projects, and celebrate successes together.

Common Tendencies of Caring

Often, when it comes to showing our care to acquaintances or to people in our professional relationships, we tend to project our own reluctance to talk. We assume that the person doesn't want their struggles acknowledged. It's tempting to leave it alone and ignore "the elephant in the room" for as long as possible. You might also be tempted to tell yourself, "Let's not get too worried," or even possibly, "This person doesn't need my help. Why should I even care?" This last thought is especially likely if you have been raised to have a traditional, "macho mentality." It is not "weak" or "unmanly" to be concerned with the people around you. Rather, that caring nature is the sign of refinement.

Another common tendency occurs when people take advantage of others who are naturally caring. These caring souls often get taken for granted. If you have ever found yourself in such a predicament, take heart. Your caring nature is not a liability or "defect." Don't be reluctant to show care in future relationships. Take the opportunity to practice self-care and set good boundaries for how you will be treated. We may not always be appreciated by others, but we owe it to ourselves to recognize our own worth and not let someone else's behaviour devalue it.

Key Quality #3 Care

The Cost of Indifference

There are grave costs connected with indifference; they affect us personally, in society, and globally. A personal sense of indifference shows up as apathy. It is a negative emotion where we lack interest or concern for our appearance, our health, or even our dreams. Given enough time, apathy kills our dreams by moving us to give up.

Social indifference has led to some of the most difficult problems of our times like bullying, political inaction, and racial tension. We may say, "That's not my problem," but that is a foolish attitude to take. Global indifference to climate concerns may very well change life on this planet forever. We cannot ignore the terrible cost of our own indifference at any scale.

However, we will soon find ourselves overwhelmed if attempting to start at a global scale. Caring begins with you and your own circle of influence. Start looking at your family, friends, and co-workers. Who are the people that you interact with on a daily basis?

When you don't care about things or people around you, it naturally follows that people around you don't want to connect with you. You have made it harder for them to form a connection with you. If you don't care, it is harder for someone to care about you. If this uncaring attitude persists, it will quickly turn you onto a very solitary path to a downward, discouraging environment.

We are born with a natural desire to express love and kindness towards others. Research shows that infants as young as 12 months will show empathy and care for others. In an experiment held at the University of Wisconsin, mothers would pretend to injure themselves with a toy hammer and pretend to cry. (The mothers kept their faces turned from the children to prevent them from picking up any cues.) The majority of the toddlers were empathetic, going over to comfort their mothers by stroking their arms and make soothing noises.[1]

There is a great benefit to caring. Helping makes others feel good and happy, and likewise, you feel happy, also. Showing someone that you genuinely care about them and showing genuine interest in the things they care about will uplift them and yourself.

The Life-Changing Power of Caring

"The simple act of caring is heroic."

—Edward Albert

Derek was a teenager in high school who was regularly bullied by one of the boys on the swim team, Logan. The near-constant harassment wore at Derek until it came to the point where he couldn't put up with it any longer. He began to get headaches and nightmares. His parents noticed a sudden change in his attitude: sullen, surly responses at home and to teachers after years of being an enthusiastic student.

---

[1] Carolyn Zahn-Waxler at the University of Wisconsin, Madison.

Key Quality #3 Care

As the loneliness and pain intensified, Derek's thoughts grew self-destructive. He began to devise a plan to kill himself. On Friday afternoon, he cleared out his locker and started to walk home with several heavy binders. As he was leaving the school, he stumbled. A binder fell to the ground, scattering papers everywhere. Another kid, Michael, saw Derek picking up his notes and walked over to help him pick up the papers.

Michael saw that Derek seemed down, so he invited Derek to hang out. They went for pizza and talked about which Star Wars movie was the best. At Michael's house, they ended up playing video games and ended up hanging out together for most of the weekend.

Eventually, Derek and Michael became good friends. Derek never followed through on his terrible plan. He had something to look forward to in his life. A simple gesture helped Derek avoid the tragic decision that he had originally planned.

In showing an interest and sticking up for Derek, Michael was caring for his friend. Derek's confidence in himself grew and he began to trust other people again. Once he felt that someone cared, he was able to find better coping strategies for dealing with school pressures and he had the courage to ask for help with the bullying problem. A simple act of kindness was life-changing for Derek. Caring has greater impact than we may ever know.

Chapter 6

Key Quality #2
RESPECT

"If you want to be a great leader, remember to treat all people with respect at all times. For one, because you never know when you'll need their help. And two, because it's a sign you respect people, which all great leaders do."

—Simon Sinek

Respect is something that is misunderstood in today's society, because it is not generally taught at home or in schools. So, let's start with a quick quiz. What is the real meaning of respect:

a. An act of giving particular attention
b. High or special regard
c. Consideration
d. Esteem

What do you think the answer is? At the end of the chapter I will reveal the answer to you.

How Does the World See Respect?

This is beneficial to understand. Media today portrays the opposite of respect. It gives lip service to it, but respect doesn't sell. By default, the media actually promotes disrespect because it makes money.

The world views respect as something that you have to earn, as opposed to something that you should just have. The sad thing is that only certain people can earn it. Respect is something that you can only have depending on your social status, and what you amounted to in life. In other words, if you are liked by your friends and are popular then you have respect, and are worthy of being shown respect.

Whereas if you are not known or are not very popular or average, the common attitude is that you are not worthy of being shown respect—which is ultimately wrong and incorrect.

Did you ever have this experience as a child? You hated going to school because you were bullied, picked on, or were just not liked for some attribute that others considered undesirable? They made your life miserable for something that you had no or very little control over.

My friend Kim felt that way growing up. She was different from the other kids. She and her sister were the only mulatto kids in a predominantly white school. She was raised by a single dad in the 70's because her Mom had passed away. She had auburn hair (which was not popular as it is today), and she was a foot taller than anyone else her age.

Everyday, she was teased, made fun of, and made to feel like she wasn't worth anything, all because she didn't fit into what society and TV considered normal. She was not respected for the gifts that she did have.

Key Quality #2 Respect

Thankfully, while Kim still remembers that time, it no longer affects her. She learned a long time ago how to respect and love herself and appreciate the wonderful gifts she has been given and to use them to create a great life.

So here is the first thing about general respect. It is not something you earn.

What is Respect?

There are three aspects to it. The first one is to honour and esteem as worthy every person on the face of the earth, just because they are a person. I know it sounds strange but if we were to treat each person that way, we would not have the problems we do on this earth.

It doesn't mean that we have to like every single person. What it does mean is that you can treat them with kindness, listen to their opinion without arguing and agree to disagree and be able to go your separate ways. Still believing that person has worth.

Respecting someone also doesn't mean that you become a doormat accepting any behavior that comes your way, because the first person that you need to respect and believe has worth is yourself. Esteeming someone as worthy, doesn't mean that you justify bad actions.

For example; someone is upset with you and verbally being mean to you. Can you show respect to yourself and them at the same time? Yes, you can by removing yourself from the situation as quickly as possible.

You may be thinking to yourself, "Shouldn't I say

something to him and correct him?" The answer is no. When you start to justify your own actions, you are showing the other person that you don't respect yourself. You are allowing the other person's disrespect to come into you.

You are showing them respect by not beating them up (though it is very tempting), and you are showing yourself respect by not allowing that person to continue to talk to you that way.

What about a less extreme example? You are having a discussion with someone and you disagree with each other. The conversation has been going on for some time, and it is going nowhere and has the potential of becoming heated. How do you deal with that situation with regard to respect?

Here are a few different things you can say. How about, "It looks like we are not going to come to middle ground on this subject. Why don't we just agree to disagree and go onto something we can agree about?" Or you can simple say, "Okay."

It acknowledges that you heard what the person said, but it doesn't necessarily agree or disagree with it. It is a neutral statement. It is especially good to use if you think that the conversation is moving towards hostility. This provides you the opportunity to change the subject to something more pleasant.

The second aspect of respect is something that this world needs to get back to, and that is consideration for a person's position. We are being taught in today's society that all authority is bad and that we should balk it whenever we can.

Key Quality #2 Respect

That includes people like police and judges, our bosses and parents. Anybody in authority above us should be stomped on, not esteemed and this is very sad.

We want our right to do whatever we want without consequence, but that is not how a healthy society works. We have amazing freedoms here in Canada and the US, but people have taken that to the extreme that there shouldn't be any rules at all. I believe that freedom should be protected, but the responsibility of freedom should be to protect what is morally and ethically right.

That is where we are seeing a breakdown in our society. Every generation is worse than the generation before. Today's generation for the most part has no respect for parents, teachers, or the law. It is a self-entitled age, where what the person wants is all that matters, even at the expense of someone else. That is horrible place to be.

There is one aspect of respect that is earned and that is when someone does something that is truly extraordinary in any category. An athlete who wins gold, an artist who paints and incredible piece of art, a scientist who discovers something that revolutionizes our world, those people deserve extra honor and esteem.

Here is the thing to understand. They are not worth more than an average person. You are not respecting them because they are more important than anyone else. You are giving the years of hard work and dedication that it took to reach that goal the respect it deserves. They paid the price that others have not and that deserves special notice.

Refine Yourself

How Does Respect Change the World?

One person at a time. Let me share a story with you. When Harry was little, he had someone who showed him disrespect all the time. If he was sitting in a room reading, the other guy would intentionally turn out the light so he couldn't see the page. He would shut off the TV while Harry was watching it. He would do everything he could to make Harry's life miserable.

I wish I could tell you that Harry showed him respect every single time, but he was a kid and still learning the power of esteem in his life. So, sometimes they would fight. Which is what the other guy wanted in the first place and they would both get into trouble. The other guy was stronger, so he won; which made Harry feel even worse about himself.

There came a day when Harry was tired of fighting and realized that he was better than that. He knew that if this was going to stop, he had to first start respecting himself and then the other guy. He thought about what he could do and he finally came up with a solution.

The next time the other guy started to do those mean things, Harry didn't react. He didn't get angry and he didn't see himself as less. He ignored him as if nothing happened at all. This made the other guy angry and for a short period of time the attacks increased, but Harry knew that they best way to respect himself was to not let it all in.

Over time the other guy got tired of no reaction, no matter what he did. He was confused because nothing he did seem to faze Harry and decided that it was too boring

Key Quality #2 Respect

and stopped, but that is when the good started to happen. Harry took it to the next level and started to show the other guy honour and thanks for his good behaviour towards him; within six months the other guy had gone from being an enemy to being Harry's protector and friend. Why? Because Harry chose to honor himself and the other guy.

So, let's go back to the start of the chapter and the quiz. What is the real meaning of respect?

a. An act of giving particular attention

b. High or special regard

c. Consideration

d. Esteem

Which answer did you choose? If you said all of them. You are right. I encourage you as part of your refinement process to include honour and respect in it. If each person was to grow in respect, we would see wide sweeping changes in this world for the better, but it always starts with one person. YOU. As you do what you need to, others see it and it encourages them to do the same.

Now the next chapter is the most powerful of all and the reason why I saved it for last and that is LOVE.

Chapter 7

Key Quality #1
LOVE

"The greatest thing you'll ever learn is just to love and be loved in return."

—Eden Ahbez

Love is an all-consuming passion that we pursue all our lives. Yet we struggle to answer the question: what is love? The answer is simultaneously obvious and elusive. Love is the topic of hundreds of books, songs, and movies. It "makes the world go around." It is a many-splendored thing. It means different things to different people. It seems pedantic to even ask the question—we know it when we see it. And yet . . .

A general definition of love is an intense feeling of deep affection towards someone or something. But within that broad definition, there are four main categories: familial, friendship, romantic and agape.

Four Types of Love

Parental or familial love is the kind of affection that most people experience first in their lives. There is a unique bond created by parenthood. Whether by birth, adoption or blending, parents demonstrate their love for their children by giving them time, attention, and (devoted) care. A parent's love will often focus on protecting, teaching, and disciplining their children in preparation for adulthood.

A parent teaches their child how to love others by demonstrating that love to their partner and their child. Kind words and thoughtful actions are like ripples from a stone thrown into a pond: they carry on much longer than the act that caused them. Being intentional in showing your family love and respect builds caring communities.

Friendship is one of life's greatest joys. If you live in a city, live to be 78, and meet an average of three people in a day, you have the potential to interact with approximately 80,000 people in your lifetime. But of that vast number, there are really only a treasured few people who we would truly count as friends. Friends are people that understand us. They "get" our sense of humour. Friends celebrate our triumphs and mourn our defeats as if those gains and losses were their own. It is a love born of empathy and trust. Friendship can grow between anyone, under the right circumstances: shared interests or experiences, even a shared dislike of something can spark a connection between friends. The deep love of friendship has been documented throughout history.

By contrast, the cultural concept of romantic love is a relatively recent idea. If you were born 200 years ago, your parents would have had a much stronger influence on the person you would ultimately marry. The end goal of a relationship was marriage and children. Matches were made

Key Quality #1 Love

to strengthen political ties, gain social standing, and secure financial interests.

Western pop culture is an endless celebration of romantic love. From the latest romantic comedy starring Ryan Gosling and Emma Stone to Katie Perry's latest top ten hit. Our attention is drawn to the pursuit of romantic love. Romantic love is intense and pleasurable. Our hormones and brain chemistry work together to create intense feelings for intimacy.

When you feel a romantic love, it is usually accompanied by an equally strong desire to express this love physically to the object of your desire. In layman's terms, you want to give your love "muchas smooches!" The ultimate goal of romantic love is to spend a lifetime partnered with the person who reflects this love back to you. In movies and novels, this type of love is considered the most desirable of all love. It is so worthy of pursuit that people will choose romantic love over career success, financial gain, even to the point of sacrificing one's other relationships with family members and friends.

The term *agape* (pronounced ah-GAP-ay) is perhaps less well-known than the other types of love, but when we do express it, we experience the best that humanity has to offer. It comes from the Greek, referring to "the love God has for man." Agape is a spiritual concept used in Christianity to express the *unconditional* quality of God's love for humanity. It is a love that is selfless, willing to sacrifice one's one comfort for the sake of another. Thomas Aquinas taught that agape is the act of "willing the good of another." This mindfulness of others requires the ability to look beyond ourselves and our own comforts. As we seek to refine ourselves, we should strive to have this kind of love for all mankind.

A Life Without Love

> *If I speak in the tongues of men and of angels, but have not love, I am a noisy gong or a clanging cymbal. And if I have prophetic powers, and understand all mysteries and all knowledge, and if I have all faith, so as to remove mountains, but have not love, I am nothing. If I give away all I have, and if I deliver up my body to be burned, but have not love, I gain nothing.*
>
> —1 Corinthians 13:1-3

Life is meaningless without love. All our accomplishments, all our knowledge and wealth become trivial pastimes without love to give our actions significance. If we choose to live our lives as though we are alone, we pay a hefty price: a life without love is no life at all.

There are serious health problems associated with experiencing a lack of affection. People who live without love are lonelier and more susceptible to stress and depression because they have less social support.

A lack of love can increase mood and anxiety disorders, causing more anti-social behaviours like people becoming closed off and avoiding interactions with others. It becomes increasingly difficult to express their thoughts and feelings. The longer this continues, the harder it is to trust or form connections with another person. Ironically, this behaviour becomes a repeating cycle that has the effect of driving people away, often at a time when they are most needed.

A lack of love tends to colour one's outlook. It weakens the ability to empathize with others. Empathy is the ability to put yourself in someone else's place and understand what they are going through, rather simply feeling sorry for them (which is sympathy). When you are able to empathize with others, you are able to approach problems from their point of view while still offering helpful solutions.

The Work of Love

One problem with the classic Hollywood love story is that it fools us into thinking that once the initial obstacles are overcome, the love relationship will be perfect. We know this before we even buy a ticket—a romantic comedy will have a happy ending. That's great, but it ignores the reality that real love is often real work.

If you find yourself rolling your eyes or shuddering at the thought of more work, or imagining of a list "dos-and-don'ts," I sympathize. But I am also going to suggest that response comes from a place of immaturity. After years of school followed by years of work, many people react unenthusiastically to the suggestion of additional work because they have learned to associate work with drudgery, or a series of pointless tasks to be completed.

Love is work, but I propose to you that rather than the

drudgery you have been imagining, it is the work of an artist perfecting his craft to capture light and life in a brushstroke. It is the work of an Olympic athlete training her body to endure to the end of the race, pushing herself to grow stronger and do better than before. Love takes practice.

True love requires you to be selfless and make sacrifices. It is second nature in parental love, where a mother will sacrifice her sleep to take care of a sick child, or a father will carry his children when they are too tired to walk. We recognize this aspect of selflessness in parental love, but it should be present in romantic love, too.

Newsflash: It's not always about you! Difficult as it may be to believe, it's true. Part of refining your character is to learn when your needs are not the greatest priority. True love will require that sometimes your wants and needs must take a back seat to the needs of someone else.

Selfless love can be seen in the example of Dale and Linda, a married couple coping with serious illness. When Linda was diagnosed with breast cancer for the second time, they were both heartbroken. But Dale would not let Linda fall into despair. "We will fight this. You are going to beat this, Linda. I know you can do it. Our love is stronger than sickness."

It won't always be easy, or pleasant. It's not fun to do laundry at 3:00 a.m. because a child threw up. It is emotionally overwhelming to watch a friend grieve the death of his mother after years of Alzheimer's. But true love does these things and more, if asked.

Key Quality #1 Love

Don't Give Up

You might find yourself in a situation where your love is being taken for granted. This is not a common tendency of love. It is a common tendency of human nature. Selfishness happens. You have probably done the same thing, on occasion. (Yes, even someone as nice as you!)

Don't be discouraged. Be loving, and ready to forgive the person who hurt you. Forgiveness must be practiced often for you to get good at it. Don't worry that you are giving in, or being "a doormat." If you love yourself, you will know the difference between an occasional thoughtlessness and a pattern of casual mistreatment. (If you have found that you do tend to let yourself be taken advantage of, ask a friend to help assess whether you are giving more than you should. Again, consider whether it is a pattern of behaviour.) Don't give up on love just because you have discovered your love is human too. You are doing the work of refining *yourself*, not anyone else.

In the Name of Love

> "Love is the only force capable of transforming an enemy into a friend."
>
> —Martin Luther King Jr.

Ann Arbor, Michigan is a liberal, multicultural city, home to people of many races and cultures. Which made it surprising that the Klu Klux Klan decided to hold a rally at city hall in June 1996. The group of white supremacists at the rally was small, compared to over three hundred protesters who gathered in opposition of the hate group.

A detachment from the Ann Arbor police force was at the city hall building. Standing by court order, they carried out their duty to serve in riot gear and with tear gas ready. They formed a protective barrier between the hooded speakers and the protesters. Keshia Thomas, an African-American high school student was also in the crowd at the rally, ready to protest the KKK.

Tensions were growing as the leader continued his poisonous message, but the yards of chain-link fence, along with the police presence seemed to be a sufficient deterrent to the threat of violence. Until the moment a woman's voice squawked over a megaphone: "There's a Klansman in the crowd!"

A middle-aged man with an SS tattoo and dressed in Confederate flag t-shirt stood among the protesters. While he did not identify himself as a KKK member, the tattoo and t-shirt marked him as sympathetic to the racist message of the group. Realizing the danger that he was in, the man turned and tried to walk away from the crowd.

"Get him!"

"Kill the Nazi!"

He began to run, but he was knocked to the ground. Lying prone, blows rained down on him. He was kicked and beaten with the sticks from the protestors. When it seemed that fate had delivered the crowd's enemy to their feet, the righteous anger was transformed into a lust for vengeance.

Key Quality #1 Love

Sometimes, our biggest decisions can take place in a matter of seconds. As she looked on in disbelief. Keshia was horrified by the violence around her. "This isn't right," she whispered to herself. She shouted, "This isn't right!" raising her voice along with other shouts of the crowd.

She threw herself over the man, covering his body with hers. Keshia shielded the man from the kicks and punches of the enraged mob.

"No! Stop it! Stop it! You can't kill hate with hate!"

Cautiously, she lowered her arm from shielding her face. Keshia looked up at the people, her eyes pleading with them to understand. "We have to choose love."

Puzzled by Keshia's compassion, the protesters shook their heads. But they held back their fists and their kicks. Slowly, the people stepped back and made a space. Keshia helped the man to his feet and walked him through the crowd.

The seeds of hate do not have to take root in our hearts. In one crucial moment, Keshia chose agape love. She could have remained safely anonymous in the crowd, but she risked her own safety for a stranger who would sooner call himself her enemy. And the world was made a better place for it.

Where is the Love?

Why is love so desperately needed in today's world? We see the need for a greater love everywhere: in our cities, where homeless people will sleep over subway grates; in our schools, where children can't concentrate on lessons because they haven't eaten; in our homes, where we would rather stream

Orange is the New Black than talk with our families. It is too easy to disconnect and disengage from the real work that is love in action. We must choose love, even when it's difficult. Love is worth the work.

Miracles happen when people decide to act with love. When people work together, love moves them to a positive "growth" mindset. The Civil Rights movement of the 1960's, projects like LIVE AID and BAND AID are examples of love's power to change the world. "Impossible" problems like homelessness, addiction, and despair can be met with compassion, kindness, and hope if we act with love.

Chapter 8

REFINEMENT

"The quality of a person's life is in direct proportion to their commitment to excellence, regardless of their chosen field of endeavour."

—Vince Lombardi

Refinement begins when you realize that you want to make a difference in your life and are willing to make the changes necessary to make your vision become a reality. Be prepared: it's going to take effort and it will be challenging. The main thing to keep in mind is the end result: the refined person that you know you can become.

In my personal journey to refinement, I have had to grow in many ways. It has been challenging, but I have seen that growth process as I continue to refine myself. Am I closing in on the final result? Of course not! But I am getting closer and closer than ever before; because refining yourself is an ongoing process, like the polishing of a rough gemstone into a sparkling gem.

My early years in the foster care system had shaped me into a robot of sorts. I protected myself by projecting a hard, cynical exterior that had been built up over years of hurt. That past experience is over. I look back from where I started to where I am now, and it is quite a big difference. Even the people who knew the old me are also able to see the difference as well.

Another resource that will speed you on the path to refinement is to read as much as you can. One of the books that helped me on my journey was reading and studying the Bible. Trying to understand it and applying the principles in my life had a significant impact on me. If you are interested in learning more, I would recommend getting a version that uses modern English like the New Living Translation (NLT) or the New International Version (NIV).

As you seek to improve yourself, look for mentors to help you further enhance your efforts. One of my mentors is Raymond Aaron. Raymond's teachings and his insights have helped me to better myself. His positive, dynamic energy has been a major influence in how I have continued to move forward with my life.

One of the best things that has happened to me since I started this process of self-refinement is how I experience other people, and how they experience *me*. Remember how I said that I was the person who could depress an entire room just by walking in the door?

Well, today, I know that I am perceived as outgoing and approachable. I have grown into a friendly, easy going guy, someone that you could converse and be relaxed with. I quite enjoy having casual conversations now; without feeling like I have to put a show on or that people will have to be careful of what they say around me.

As I have honed my ability to empathize and care for other people. I have found that many people have felt that they are able to confide in me as if they were talking to a close friend, somebody they known for years. Naturally, I am making deeper and long-lasting friendships.

After years of protecting myself, I have found that I am more open to initiate conversations about my past. Since working with Raymond Aaron and beginning the process of self-refinement, I have been more open and approachable, as well as more outgoing.

The Work of a Lifetime

A life of refinement is an ongoing process, but you will discover that your progress is not a straight line from Point A to Point B. As you work on your strengths and weaknesses, remember that you are doing the work to become a skilled craftsman. There will be days when you think that nothing is happening, and other days when everything just seems to fall into place. Be patient and monitor your personal journey to refinement, perhaps by keeping a journal or a blog.

Meaningful changes happen when you make goals and regularly track your progress. Start by assessing where you are today. Answer the questions honestly, but without judgement or self-crimination. This isn't a test to see how 'bad' or 'good' you are. You are just 'taking your temperature' to figure out where you are starting from.

After you have answered the questions, try implementing the action steps that follow and retake the test after 30 days of working on each key characteristic of refinement. You will be surprised to see how you have grown.

#6 Forgiveness Assessment

It's time to choose to move past former injuries and hurt feelings. Release yourself from anger and the trap of holding grudges. Negative thoughts and anger will cause you pain, both physically and mentally. When you refine your ability to forgive, you become a calmer, happier person. Why hold on to your hurt when you can experience the peace that forgiveness brings?

Ask yourself:

1. Do you find it difficult to forgive people who have offended you?
2. Is there a past offense that you have not forgiven?
3. Are you angry about something today?
4. Have you offended someone and not yet asked their forgiveness?
5. Do you need to forgive yourself for past mistakes?

Action Steps to Forgiveness

Make a conscious decision today that you are letting go of these feelings and forgiving the person(s) who have hurt you in the past. Say the words aloud, "I forgive [NAME] for hurting me. I release them and I release my anger." Do this every time

If possible (and safe for you to do so), meet with the person to forgive them face-to-face. Some people find it helpful to

Refinement

write letters (not necessarily to send) to express themselves more completely.

#5 Communication Skills Assessment

Communication is what draws people together. You need clear communication to express your ideas, fears, and deepest needs. Consider the people to whom you feel closest. Think of how you would like to strengthen your friendship with that person.

1. Could you ask a stranger to change $20 bill?
2. Could you hold a conversation with someone if you were stuck in an elevator?
3. Who is your best friend?
4. Imagine that you just landed your dream job. Who would you call to tell the good news?
5. Imagine that you got a flat tire at 2:00 A.M., and you don't have CAA. Who is the friend that you could count on to help you out?

Action Steps to Better Communication

Practice striking up conversations with new people, or people you don't know all that well. Begin making connections in the workplace by asking coworkers about their weekend or their special interests. (Of course, your employer will prefer that you save longer conversations for lunch breaks!)

Don't worry if you know nothing about their interests.

People love it when you ask them about their passions. ("I had no idea that you were into making paper airplanes/playing Minecraft/baking cupcakes!") Ask them, "What got you started?" and follow up with "What is your favourite part?" Even if you don't find the topic personally appealing, you can always say, "It sounds like you really enjoy it."

#4 Trust Assessment

While we can't simply assign a number to rank a person's trustworthiness, we can listen to what our intuition tells us. Remember, trust comes from living with mind at peace.

1. Who can you share your personal secrets, without fear that they will disclose a confidence?
2. What do you put your trust in? Friendship? Money? Faith?
3. Do you catch yourself telling "little white lies"?
4. What are the ways that you are trustworthy?
5. Are there areas of your life where you wish to be more reliable?

Action Steps to Building Greater Trust

Begin with credibility. Start listening to yourself closely and pay attention to when you exaggerate. When you tell people about your day, do you find yourself recounting events in ways that cast yourself as the hero or the victim? Both are pitfalls. Become impeccable with your word. How good are your promises? If you want to become known for reliability, be cautious about promising more than you can deliver. Better that you say "No," than to disappoint because you have not given the time and care to fulfill a request to the best of your abilities.

#3 Caring Assessment

Caring is the act of uplifting others. It is the ability to show love and compassion, even when you have been hurt. Making the choice to get involved with others and engaging in projects to help those less fortunate builds community and benefits society.

1. What moves your heart?
2. Who are the people in need in your community?
3. Can you ask your employer to partner with a charitable organization to give back to the community?

Action Steps to Practicing Care

Find a non-profit organization that needs help and volunteer your time. You have skills that can help others grow. Do you like working with kids? Maybe being a Big Brother or Big Sister is a good fit. Are you crazy about sports? Coaching and refereeing are also possibilities that would enable you to show that you care.

#2 Respect Assessment

Respect is showing honour to others. **All** people have value. Practice the Golden Rule: treat every person the way you want to be treated. Look for what is worthy of esteem in everyone, including yourself. Surface differences like appearance, race, gender, or age should not affect the respect you give to everyone.

1. Who do you respect socially?
2. Who do you respect in the workplace?
3. What kind of actions would make you lose respect for someone?

Action Steps to Greater Respect

Recognize others' achievements, and celebrate your own. You cannot demand respect, or force it from other people, but you can take a firm stand when you feel you are being disrespected. Do not give in to disrespectful suggestions. Teach people how to treat you by indicating what kind of treatment you will not tolerate.

Show respect for people who have been given authority. It is courteous. You may not necessarily share all the same opinions (in fact, you probably won't!) but this person has been given an opportunity to lead. Show them the respect that you would wish to experience in their place.

Refinement

#1 Love Assessment

The big one is always Love. Look for ways to practice all four types of love, but especially Agape love - **unconditional love.** Love is the cord intertwined with every other aspect of refinement.

1. Who do you love?
2. How do you show your love?
3. Think of your friends, family, and romantic partner. How would these people describe the way you love?
4. What would it look like if you could share your love with the world?

Action Steps to Creating a World of Love

Start by speaking kindly to people. Every day, everyone you meet, everywhere you go. Thank people, especially people in the service industry. Help someone by holding the door for them. Pay a sincere compliment to your coworkers.

Practice patience with other people. They might not understand what you are trying to do and will be suspicious. (Especially if it seems to them that you are making a big change!)

Finally, I encourage you to think of your own refinement process as a journey to personal excellence that you travel every day. May you begin a lifetime of deeper and richer relationships at home and in the workplace, each one built on a foundation of integrity and trust, bound by love.

It Starts Here

I hope that this book has been of help to you. Believe it or not, writing this book has been part of my refinement process and has helped me to see life clearer. Now my goal is to help others including you.

If you have read this book and recognized within yourself a need to change, but know that you can't do it on your own, then I encourage you to reach out to me and let's see how we can work together to make your life what you want it to be.

You can connect with me by visiting dennisgarrido.com and we can discuss your next steps.

Wishing You A Life Full Of Good Things,
Dennis Garrido

www.ingramcontent.com/pod-product-compliance
Lightning Source LLC
Chambersburg PA
CBHW050655160426
43194CB00010B/1950